Trading Options for Beginners

© Copyright 2018 by Stephan Marchini & David Marchini All rights reserved.

The following e-book is reproduced below with the goal of providing information that is as accurate and reliable as possible. Regardless, purchasing this e-book can be seen as consent to the fact that both the publisher and the author of this book are in no way experts on the topics discussed within and that any recommendations or suggestions that are made herein are for entertainment purposes only. Professionals should be consulted as needed prior to undertaking any of the action endorsed herein.

This declaration is deemed fair and valid by both the American Bar Association and the Committee of Publishers Association and is legally binding throughout the United States.

Furthermore, the transmission, duplication or reproduction of any of the following work including specific information will be considered an illegal act irrespective of if it is done electronically or in print. This extends to creating a secondary or tertiary copy of the work or a recorded copy and is only allowed with express written consent from the Publisher. All additional rights reserved.

The information in the following pages is broadly considered to be a truthful and accurate account of facts and as such any inattention, use or misuse of the information in question by the reader will render any resulting actions solely under their purview. There are no scenarios in which the publisher or the original author of this work can be in any fashion deemed liable for any hardship or damages that may befall them after undertaking information described herein.

Additionally, the information in the following pages is intended only for informational purposes and should thus be thought of as universal. As befitting its nature, it is presented without assurance regarding its prolonged validity or interim quality. Trademarks that are mentioned are done without written consent and can in no way be considered an endorsement from the trademark holder.

Table of Contents

Introduction
Chapter 1: What Are Options?
  What Are Options?
  Understanding Options
    When Should You Use Options?
    Derivatives
    Types of Options
    Example of How Options Work
    Another Example—Call Option
  Learn About Buying and Selling Call and Put Options
    Long Position
    Short Position
  Further Example of Options Application
Chapter 2: Fundamentals of Options Trading
  Other Terminologies Used in Options Trading
  Terms Describing an Option's Value
  Options Seller and Buyer Terms
Chapter 3: Basic Options Trading Strategies
  1. The Long Call Options Trading Strategy
    Potential Benefits and Downsides
    Why Adopt This Strategy?
  2. The Long Put Options Trading Strategy

    What Are the Potential Losses or Benefits?

    Why Use This Strategy?

3. The Short Put Options Trading Strategy

    Potential Benefits and Downsides

    Why Apply this Strategy?

4. The Covered Call Options Trading Strategy

    Any Potential Benefits or Cons?

    When Is This Strategy Adopted?

5. The Married Put Option Strategy

    Potential Benefits and Downsides of This Strategy

Chapter 4: How to Trade Options

    Caution

    Reading Options Symbols, Chains, and Tables

An Introduction to Options Chains

Various Types of Options Chains

    The Basic Call and Put Options Chain

    The Options Strategies Chain

    Call and Put Options Pricer

    Call and Put Option Matrix

The Basic Call and Put Options Chain

The Call and Put Options Pricer

Options Strategies Chains

Call and Put Options Matrix

Learn About Options Pricing

What Are Extrinsic and Intrinsic Values?
Calculating Intrinsic Value
    Extrinsic Value
  Other Considerations of Stock Option Pricing
    Strike Price
    How to Price Options
  How to Read Options Quotes
    Option Volume and Open Interest
    Expiration Cycles
    Expiration Dates
  Trading Options
    How to Buy Call Options
    Buying Put Options
Chapter 5: Risks That You Need to Avoid
  Understanding Options Risks
  Time Is Not on Your Side
  Prices Can Move Pretty Fast
  Naked Short Positions Can Result in Substantial Losses
Chapter 6: Choosing a Broker
  Mistakes that You Need to Avoid
    Problems Pertaining to the Price Tag
    Manage Both Greed and Fear
    Properly Allocate Funds to Trades
  Identifying a Reliable Broker

Conclusion

Introduction

Congratulations on downloading *Trading Options for Beginners* and thank you for doing so.

This book will discuss options and how to trade in them so you will know some ways on how you can earn a great profit. You will be introduced to options, understand how they function, and the power behind them.

Options can earn you serious profits when you invest in relatively small amounts of money compared to buying shares directly. Instead of buying shares, you will learn how to spread your money and invest it in options. While the profit margins are astronomical, there are certain risks involved. Fortunately, this book will teach you about the risks and how you can possibly avoid them.

There are plenty of books on this subject, which you can easily find on the market. Thanks again for choosing this one! Every effort was made to ensure it is full of as much useful information as possible. Please enjoy!

Chapter 1: What Are Options?

There are plenty of ways of growing your money. Investing in different products at the securities exchange is one of the most trusted ways of getting rich. Some of the traditional ways of investing funds include buying and selling shares, investing in bonds and other securities.

However, if you really want to grow your wealth, then you should move away from traditional investments and move to more lucrative stock market instruments. For instance, you should invest your funds in options to grow your wealth much faster and by larger amounts.

A lot of investors have heard of terms such as derivatives, strike price, bull call spreads, among others. They have even heard of options but are not sure what they are and how they work. Fortunately, options are not that difficult to understand. Let us examine them closely in order to gain deeper insights.

What Are Options?

An option is simply a contract that allows you the opportunity to sell or buy 100 shares of a particular stock at an agreed price and a set date. Options grant you the right to buy or sell the stock, but you are never obligated to do so.

There are call options and put options. A put option grants you the rights to sell an underlying security while a call option awards you the right to buy an underlying security.

If you choose to exercise your right to buy or sell an underlying security, then you will have to do so within the stipulated time period and at the set price. If you wish, then you can forego the right, and the option will expire. At the very least, you will only have lost the cost of setting it up.

Understanding Options

Options may sound complex but are pretty easy to understand if you pay keen attention. You will come across numerous traders' profiles with different security types including bonds, stocks, mutual funds, ETFs, and even options.

Options are another asset class. If applied correctly, they will offer numerous benefits that all other assets on their own cannot. For instance, you can use options to hedge against negative outcomes like a declining stock market or falling oil prices. You can use options to generate recurrent income and for speculative purposes like wagering on the movement of a stock.

When Should You Use Options?

As an investor, you will have a number of opportunities to use options. However, there is a number that is truly beneficial. Here is a brief look at them.

- Options buy you time if you need to sit back and watch things develop.
- You require very little funds to invest in options compared to buying shares.
- Options will offer you protection from losses because they lock in price but without the obligation to buy.

Always keep in mind that options offer no free ride or a free lunch. Trading in options carries some risks due to their predictive nature. Any prediction will turn out one way or another. The good news here is that any losses that you incur will only be equivalent to the cost of setting up the option. This cost is significantly lower than buying the underlying security.

Derivatives
Options are a kind of derivative. Investors are often talking about different derivatives. Options derive their value from an underlying stock or security. In fact, options belong to the class of securities known as derivatives. For a long time, people associated derivatives with high-risk investments. This notion is not really true.

Derivatives obtain their value from an underlying security. Think about wine, for instance. Wine is produced from grapes. We also have ketchup which is derived from tomatoes. This is basically how derivatives function.

Types of Options
A lot of the time, people hear of options and think of stock options. However, options can be written on just about all kinds of financial products. These include commodities, currencies, bonds, stock indices, futures contracts, and much more.

When it comes to stock options, there are only certain types that are accepted for options trading and not all. For a company's stock to qualify, it must meet certain qualifying criteria. The criterion is set by the exchange where the stock is traded. As long as the criterion is set, the stock will be eligible. However, when it fails, it gets disqualified.

Example of How Options Work
Let us assume that there is a company whose stock you wish to buy because you believe the price will rise. What you need to do is set up an option. Since your plan is to buy stock, then you will choose a call option.

A call option grants you the right to purchase a security at a later date at an agreed price. Let us assume that the stock you are interested in will see a gain in price in three months. The option will give you the right to buy the stock at this price for the next three months.

You will be charged a fee for the option. The cost of the option is usually $1 or $2 for every 100 shares. So you will pay a price of about $100 if you intend to purchase 10,000 shares. If the current price of the share is $5, you can lock the price at probably $5.50. Let us say that in three months' time, this price rises to $8.50. You will still buy the stock at $5.50, saving yourself plenty of money. You could then sell the shares at the stock market and make a profit of $3 * 10,000.

Another Example—Call Option
A call option can also be considered as insurance for future use. For instance, let us assume you wish to purchase a home in the future then you notice a new development coming up. You can decide that you wish to have the right to purchase a home on the development. However, you wish to peg your decision on the development of additional amenities in the area such as schools, parks, malls, and so on. It is possible that an airport could be put up or a garbage dump.

Such decisions can help you decide whether or not to invest your money in the development. So you speak to the developer and make him a suggestion. That should certain amenities be built in the area, then you will purchase an apartment at perhaps $350,000 within three years. The property developer may agree with you but will not grant you this for free. He will charge you a fee for this, probably 1% of the home's value or $3,500.

Suppose that after three years, the development is complete, and the amenities you desired were put up. You will then approach the property developer and exercise your right to buy property at the agreed price. By this time, the price of an apartment is probably double at $700.000. You will have saved yourself a whopping $350,000 by using options. In any instance, the property developer will keep the $3,500 which was the cost of setting up the option.

Let us assume that a different situation happens, and the city neglects to put up the desired amenities but instead puts up a dumping site. If you decide to forego your right to purchase an apartment, then you will be free to do so. However, you will lose the price of the contract which in our case is $3,500. This is a relatively small price to lose yet the benefits you stand to gain are significantly high.

Learn About Buying and Selling Call and Put Options

Long Position
When you buy stock, you get what is known as a long position. When you buy a call option, you get into a potential long position based on the underlying stock.
On the other hand, when you sell a stock short, then you are short selling. This essentially gives you a short position. Short selling means that you sell at a loss while long selling implies a profit. When you sell a naked call or an uncovered call, you will enter a potentially short position based on the underlying stock.

Short Position
You enter into a potential short position based on the underlying stock when you purchase a put option. Should you sell a naked put, you will enter a potential long position relative to the underlying stock.

If you can understand these four positions and keep them in mind, then you will easily understand the intricacies of selling and buying options. Ideally, you can buy call options and put options as well as sell call options and put options.

Holders: Anyone who buys options is generally referred to as an options holder.
Writers: A person who sells an option is generally referred to as an options writer.

Call and put holders are also known as buyers. They have the right to buy options but are not obligated to do so. They can exercise this right but only within the stipulated time and under the agreed conditions. This way, call and put holders only suffer losses equivalent to the premium charged for the options contract.

Call and put writers are sellers. They have an obligation to sell options or buy should the option expire and the contract makes money. Therefore, sellers are always expected to oblige to the buyer's wishes. This exposes them to more risks. Therefore, writers stand to lose a lot more than just the cost of writing the options contract.

Further Example of Options Application

Let us say there is a company that you really like, and you would like to own its shares. According to your predictions, the stock price is going to rise. For instance, the current stock price of this company is $25, but you believe the price will be $35 in a year's time. You can purchase a call option that will grant you the rights to purchase the stock.

On the contract, you can agree on a price of about $27 within the next one year. This contract will probably cost you about $1 per 100 shares. Now if the price does get to $35 as predicted, then you can exercise your right to buy the shares at $27. However, if the price remains constant or falls, you will not be obliged to buy, and the only loss you will incur is the options fee.

Chapter 2: Fundamentals of Options Trading

If you are to successfully trade in options, then you really need to understand basic terminology. Learning a couple of key terms will enable you to become more conversant with options. Here is a look at the key terms that are essential for options trading.

Options type: There are generally two types of options that you can sell or buy. These are call options and put options.

Strike price: The strike price is also known as the exercise price. This is the price that you will sell or buy the underlying stock should you choose to exercise your options.

Expiration date: The options contract is not indefinite and has an expiration date. The expiration date refers to the date when the contract entered into becomes void or expires.

Premium: This term refers to the price you pay for the option. This price is charged per share which means it will depend on the number of shares you sign up to. Premium has different components to it. These are the intrinsic value and time value of an option.

Intrinsic value: This is the value of an option and refers to the difference between the underlying stock's strike price and its current market price.

Time value: The time value of a share refers to the amount of time that is available before an options contract expires. The time value decreases as the expiry date approaches.

Time decay: This is the term used to express the approach of the expiration date. As this time decay progresses, the time value of an option decreases. Time decay is also commonly referred to as "theta". This time is derived from the pricing model that was used to calculate it. Time is very valuable to investors hence the importance of time decay.

Other Terminologies Used in Options Trading

Listed options: A listed option is any option that qualifies for trading at a national trading platform like the Chicago Board Options Exchange (CBOE). A listed option generally represents 100 shares of a particular stock. Such an option with 100 shares is also referred to as 1 contract. Each contract has fixed expiration dates and strike prices.

In the money: A call option is said to be in the money when the share price exceeds the strike price. On the other hand, a put option is said to be in the money anytime the share price falls below the strike price.

The price or total cost of any option is referred to as the premium. It is affected by a number of factors including volatility, time value, strike price, and stock price.

Contract names: Options contracts do have names or options symbols similar to ticker symbols for stocks.

Ask price: This is the asking price that a seller will accept to trade the option. Basically, should you wish to purchase options, then this would be the premium that you would pay.

Volume: This refers to the total number of contracts that get traded in one day.

Change: This refers to the difference in price from the previous to the current trading period. Sometimes, change is expressed in terms of percentage.

Volatility: Volatility is simply the measure of a stock's price swing measured between the low and high prices of each day. For a long time, volatility has been measured using past data.

IV, also known as implied volatility, measures the likelihood that a market considers a stock will experience significant price swing. There are certain tools that are used to measure some of these parameters. One of these is Vega. Vega is a pricing model that calculates the theoretical effect of a single point change on implied volatility.

When the implied volatility is high, it means options prices will be high due to the potential upside for the options contract. It is good to keep in mind that volatility measurements are only estimates and never accurate. They are mostly predictions on the expected change of an option's price.

Employee stock option: While these are not readily available for all traders, they are a type of call option. Plenty of listed companies offer stock options to their treasured and talented staff members, especially management, in order to retain them for a long period of time.

Employee stock options are very similar to ordinary stock options as a holder receives the right, but not the obligation, to purchase stocks at a certain price and within a stipulated time period. However, the contract only exists between the company owners or board and an employee. Others cannot trade or exchange it at the options stock markets.

This is different, however, if the options are listed. A listed option represents a contract between two different parties. This contract is completely unrelated to the company and easily be traded at the markets.

Terms Describing an Option's Value

We do not describe an option's performance as up, down, or level. This kind of description is not sufficient. Instead, we can definite performance in one of three distinct ways.

In the money: An option that has intrinsic value is said to be in the money. Basically, anytime that a stock's price in the stock market and the strike price both favor the contract owner, then the option contract is said to be in the money. Essentially, it is beneficial to the call option owner when the stock price is greater than the strike price. On the other hand, a put option is said to be in the money when the price of the stock is less than the strike price.

Out of the money: An option is said to be out of the money when there is absolutely no monetary gain expected in exercising it. This means it is a lot less lucrative or financially viable to sell stocks and shares at the strike price than it would in the general securities market. Therefore, we say that a call option is out of the money is the strike price is higher than the stock price. A put option, on the other hand, is said to be out of the money anytime that the stock price is high than the strike price.

At the money: Sometimes, the strike price is just about equal to the stock price. In such a situation, we say that the option is at the money.

Options Seller and Buyer Terms

There are special terms used to refer to options traders. In other situations, we'd refer to the traders as buyers and sellers. However, when it comes to options trading, a more technical term is used.

Writer: The term writer refers to an investor who holds an options contract and sells it. When the writer sells the option, they will receive a premium from the buyer. The buyer will be buying the right to buy a specific amount of shares at a strike price.

Holder: A holder is basically an investor seeking to purchase an options contract. A call options holder will buy an options contract and gain the right to purchase the underlying stock under stipulated terms. A put holder possesses all the rights to sell the underlying stock.

A holder and a writer are generally on opposite sides of an options transaction. One writes an option while the other signs up to it. However, the main difference between these two is the kind of losses they are exposed to.

Holders sign up to get the right to purchase or sell shares but without the obligation. The contract that they sign up to grants them the choice of if and when to exercise their right. If the option, over time, becomes out of the money, then they have the freedom to abandon the contract and let it expire. In such an instance, they will only lose the premium paid to set up the options contract.

On the other hand, things are a little different. For instance, writers lack this kind of flexibility. If a call options holder decides to exercise their right, then the writer is obligated to accept the order and execute it by selling the stock at the current strike price. Should the writer not be in possession of all the shares in a contract, then he or she will have to purchase these at current market rates and sell to the holder at the strike price. If there are any losses to be incurred, the writer is obligated to take on them.

Since the risks are pretty high for writers, it is recommended that beginners confine themselves to only buy stock options until they gather sufficient experience over the years.

Options Table

Calls for January 20, 2017 ← ———————————————————— Expiration date

Strike	Contract Name	Last Price	Bid	Ask	Change	% Change	Volume	Open Interest	Implied Volatility
15.00	170120C00015000	95.50	95.05	97.10	0.00	0.00%	4	4	318.65%
17.50	170120C00017500	88.00	89.60	90.35	0.00	0.00%	122	0	0.00%
20.00	170120C00020000	92.06	88.50	89.40	0.00	0.00%	30	0	165.23%
25.00	170120C00025000	86.97	83.45	84.40	0.00	0.00%	7	0	143.75%
30.00	170120C00030000	79.18	79.10	79.60	0.00	0.00%	1	1	117.97%
35.00	170120C00035000	70.60	72.20	72.90	0.00	0.00%	17	0	0.00%
40.00	170120C00040000	65.61	67.25	67.95	0.00	0.00%	17	0	0.00%
45.00	170120C00045000	67.05	63.55	64.50	0.00	0.00%	13	0	96.68%
47.50	170120C00047500	64.55	61.05	62.00	0.00	0.00%	10	0	91.21%
50.00	170120C00050000	61.40	60.90	61.55	1.20	1.99%	21	1,566	134.16%

- Strike price
- Contract name (stock symbol blocked out here)
- Bid / Ask
- Option volume
- Open interest

Chapter 3: Basic Options Trading Strategies

There are plenty of varied trading strategies that can be used to trade options. These range from the very simple trades to the absolute complex and exotic trades. However, regardless of how simple or how complex a trade is, it is essentially based on the basic call and put options.

Options trading can be a complex affair. It is definitely more complex compared to traditional stock trading. Ideally, when buying stocks, you will determine how many shares you want and at what price then you will fill out a form so the broker can process your order. When it comes to options trading, you will need these and a lot more.

We shall first examine the five most basic strategies. These very basic strategies used only one option. Investors refer to them as one-legged strategies. While the strategies may be simple, they are by no means risk-free. They simply provide beginners with some of the best and easy ways to get started trading options.

The Five Basic Options Trading Strategies:

- The long call
- The short put
- The long put
- The married put
- The covered call

1. The Long Call Options Trading Strategy

The long call options strategy refers to the strategy in which you purchase a call option. Buying a call option implies going long. When you go long, you expect the underlying stock's price will rise and you stand to make a profit. Let us look at an example of this strategy.

> *Example:*
> We have shares of company ABC trading at $50 per share and a call option with a $50 strike. The cost or premium of this share is $5, and the expiry period is after six months. Our options contract, in this case, is for 100 shares so the total premium cost is $5 * 100 = $500.

Potential Benefits and Downsides

Now you stand to benefit in a major way from this contract. For instance, if you time this call well, then your profits are almost infinite. This is as long as the stock price keeps moving higher. You could easily make profits of $5,000 or more in just a short while. However, the downside is that you stand to lose your premium of $500. This is the maximum loss you stand to lose should share price take a nosedive. Even then, you can still recoup some of these losses if you sell the stock before the expiration date. Therefore, the benefit of using the long call strategy is that your losses are limited, but the upside or profitability is virtually unlimited.

Why Adopt This Strategy?

There are a number of reasons why you may adopt this strategy. First, if you are not too concerned about losing the entire premium, then you are able to leverage your predictions of the stock price rising so that you stand to earn much more than directly owning the stock.

You can use this strategy to limit your risk of owning a stock directly. Owning the stock directly can expose you to potential losses while using this strategy limits your risk of loss. Instead of owning a large number of shares from one company, some traders may prefer this approach.

Also, owning a stock directly requires a lot of financial resources compared to just using an option trading strategy. Remember that owning shares means buying them directly at face value, but trading using stock options only requires payment of a premium.

2. The Long Put Options Trading Strategy

The long put trading strategy is very similar to the long call strategy. The only difference here is that you will be hoping that the stock price declines. Stock prices can rise or fall depending on a number of factors. If your predictions or analysis indicate that a stock price will fall, then your best options strategy is the long put.

As an investor, you will buy a put option and then hope that your predictions are correct. Again, if your predictions are correct, then you stand to gain unlimited profits while your losses will be limited to the cost of setting up the option. This is best demonstrated through an example.

Example:
Let us take company ABC whose stock has a current market value of $50 per share. According to your prediction, or analysis, the share price will fall in the next six months. Based on this, you discover there is a put option at $50 strike price that is currently available at $5 per 100 shares. This option has an expiration period of six months.

Now the call option charges $5 per 100 shares. If you intend to invest in 100 units of shares, then you will pay a premium of $5 * 100 = $500. Your cost and potential loss will therefore, be limited only to this amount. However, should your predictions come true then you stand to benefit much, much more.

What Are the Potential Losses or Benefits?
If you invest in a long put option trade, then you stand to benefit should your predictions turn out right. You will benefit the most if the share price falls to zero or $0 per share. When this happens, you stand to make $50 * 100 = $5,000.

Now should the price of the stock rise, you can still sell and recoup some of the funds paid for the premium. This helps minimize your losses. However, the maximum amount of losses that you stand to incur is $500 or the cost of the premium.

Why Use This Strategy?
This specific strategy provides an excellent opportunity to wager against an expected stock decline. Should the stock price decline be significant, then you stand to make much more money than through direct investment in the same stock. This is, therefore, one reason why you would wish to invest in a long put option.

There are traders who would wish to use this strategy in order to limit any possible losses arising from price fluctuations. For instance, if the price of a stock falls drastically, then the losses can be huge for any investor. However, mitigating the losses is possible with a long put option. The option provides a better alternative to short selling as the risk is high as the price of a stock could rise indefinitely.

3. The Short Put Options Trading Strategy
Yet another basic strategy that is commonly used to trade options is the short put. This strategy is basically the opposite of the long put. Remember that with the short put, an investor is betting on the price of a stock rising. With this approach, you will be selling put options which is also known as going short.

This specific strategy is pegged on the chance that the price of a particular stock will either rise or stay level until the expiry of the option. It is expected that with this strategy, the option will expire worthless, and as the seller, you will earn a premium for absolutely free. This strategy, just like the long call strategy, can be set up as a strategy to mitigate a rising stock though there are some significant differences.

Potential Benefits and Downsides

Like with all other strategies, there are potential benefits and downsides to this particular strategy. A long call basically counts on a major rise in stock price, the short put option is a little more modest, and the payoff is also modest. For instance, the long call has the capacity to return the original investment multiple times; the best that you can hope for with this specific strategy is 100% of the premium paid. In our case, this would mean keeping the entire $500 paid to you by an investor.

Now, remember three different events are likely to take place. Basically, the stock price could rise, descend, or stay the same. Now should the stock stay at the strike price or rise above it, you get to keep the full premium amount. Remember that this is your aim with this strategy.

However, should the stock fall below the strike price at expiration of the contract, then the stock will have to be purchased at a loss. The maximum loss that will be incurred should the stock price fall to $0 is $5,000.

Why Apply this Strategy?

There are a couple of reasons why traders pursue this strategy. The short put strategy is largely used by investors who strongly believe, based on insights, past data or analysis, that the stock price will go down. It is quite similar to someone seeking insurance because a seller will try to sell the premium so that they do not eventually have to pay any money should things not work out.

This strategy of selling short puts should be sparingly used because it almost always ends up with investors buying shares, yet this was not a part of the initial plan. Any stock whose price begins to fall can very easily deplete any premiums that are received from the sale of put options.

Investors sometimes adopt this strategy with the hope that the underlying stock's value will rise especially because the trade does not require any immediate financial input. However, this strategy is capped, which means your profits are limited, and any downfall experienced is quite substantial. Therefore, always proceed with caution whenever you consider using the short put strategy.

You can also use this strategy to receive a preferred buy price when the stocks are too costly. You can do this by selling put options based on an underlying stock with a low strike price. The low price is likely to attract buyers who would love to invest in the stock. For instance, let us take company ABC whose stock price is $50. You can sell put options at a price of $2 per share for a strike price of $40.

In this case, if the stock price falls below the strike price upon expiration, you will receive the stock. The investor, on the other hand, will pay $40 per share, which is the strike price, less $2 per share which is the premium already paid.

However, should the stock price stay above the indicated strike price upon expiration, then you get to keep the premium payment and repeat the same strategy all over again.

4. The Covered Call Options Trading Strategy

This is yet another basic trading strategy that is sometimes used by both traders and investors. The difference here is that this specific strategy consists of two distinct parts. As an investor, you will need to first own the underlying shares then create a call option based on the underlying stock and sell it.

You will basically award the buyer all the benefit of price appreciation above the indicated strike price. When applying this strategy, you will assume that the stock price is likely to go down slightly remain flat until expiration. This will, in essence, allow you to keep the premium paid by the buyer and also keep the shares.

As the investor, you will not only keep the stock, but you are free to repeat the process and write another call option if you so wish. There is a critical point that you need to note, though. For every 100 shares that you own, you will only be selling one single call. If you do not do this, then you will probably fall victim to short or naked calls and exposure to huge, uncapped losses in the event of the stock price rising.

Covered calls can transform an otherwise unpleasant option strategy, such as one with naked calls, into one that is safe for you and potentially rewarding. This is why sometimes this strategy is among the favorite for investors seeking to earn a regular income.

Any Potential Benefits or Cons?

Your profitability in this instance is limited to the premium paid by the buyer. In our case, the maximum premium amount is $500, so this is the maximum amount that you stand to gain should everything work out in your benefit. This will need the stock to remain at strike price or below.

However, should the stock price go up exceeding the strike price, then the option becomes a lot more expensive because it offsets most of the gains made by the stock. It also caps the upside which can mean low chances of profitability. Since the upside of this strategy is capped, you stand a high chance of suffering losses.

The problem here is that these are losses you would not have incurred had you not set up this option call. However, you do not get to lose any newly invested capital. The other challenge with this strategy is that you risk a complete loss of the stock's worth minus the $500 premium paid to you.

When Is This Strategy Adopted?
You can use the covered call option if you are an investor seeking to generate income but with limited risk even as you hope the share price will remain flat or fall just a bit until expiration.

You can also use the covered call strategy in order to get a higher sale price for your stocks. You can do this by lowering the premium cost as well as setting lucrative higher strike price. These will entice potential buyers to actually decide to purchase the call option. For instance, if the price of the stock of company ABC is $50, you can price these at a strike price of $60 then place a premium on each share of $2.

5. The Married Put Option Strategy
The married put options trading strategy is considered sophisticated, just like the covered call option strategy. Both are thought to be more sophisticated compared to other basic options trading strategies.

This specific strategy is considered more complex because it combines two approaches. These are ownership of the underlying stock and a long put. It is these two that are "married together" and hence the name of the strategy. It is important to note the implications of adopting this or any other strategy.

With the married put, you get to purchase one put for every 100 shares of stock. This particular strategy allows you, as an investor, to own shares and hope to benefit from a rise in price.

It then goes further and offers you an opportunity to hedge your position should the stock price start to fall. This approach is quite similar to purchasing insurance as it charges you a premium to protect your investment from loss due to a decline in share price.

Potential Benefits and Downsides of This Strategy

The married put has some upsides to it. However, these depend on what happens to the stock price. Should this specific strategy allow you to continue with stock ownership as the price increases, then your profit level is potentially unlimited. All you will do is deduct the cost of the premium from your profits.

The option itself will benefit you if the price of the stock falls. This will essentially match any price decline and will offset stock loss less the premium which is capped at $500. As an investor, you are able to hedge against losses and keep holding the shares in the hope that the value will appreciate once the expiration date is attained.

The benefit of this specific put option strategy is that you can use it to hedge. As an investor, you will use this specific strategy if you are hoping that your stock price continues to appreciate. You also use the marriage put option when hoping to protect price gains that your stock makes as you hope and wait for further gains.

Chapter 4: How to Trade Options

As an investor or even a trader, you should know how to trade options. You should aim to ensure that you have a certain percentage of your investment funds are committed to options trading. Options do not just diversify your portfolio but they also provide you with immense opportunities of earning large profits with minimal income.

A lot of traders, both small and large, prefer options trading to grow their wealth and benefit from higher profits. This is achievable with relatively small amounts of funds. The profits earned via options are disproportionately large compared to the investments made. One benefit of this type of trading is that you are able to begin small and grow large very fast. With amounts as little as $80, a small retail trader is able to invest in options and see gains very soon.

Option trading is a very versatile process. This opens up a whole new world of opportunities. You could use options basically to trade and earn profits, for leverage and also as insurance or protection against potential losses. All these can be attained conveniently and very quickly.

Caution
Because trading in options is a very powerful process, it is also a very risky one. It is also very dangerous and can get out of hand if not handled carefully. It is crucial that traders and investors understand exactly how to trade options and lots of other details. Getting sufficient knowledge and enough practice is crucial if you are to be successful and consistently profitable.

Reading Options Symbols, Chains, and Tables

Before you can begin trading options, you need to understand the process of buying and selling. You also need to learn how to read tables where options or quotes are printed. There are symbols used when quoting options and tables that consist of a complex array of numbers.

An Introduction to Options Chains

When you want to buy stocks, you have to check prices on a stock quote. A stock quote generally indicates listed stocks and the latest price of each stock. Similarly, if you wish to purchase options, you will check the prices on an options chain.

An options chain is basically a table that lists or outlines the total number of available options based on qualifying stocks. The chain is presented in a number of different ways so learning how to read it is crucial. You should learn how to read an options chain accurately and precisely. This is the very first step if you are to successfully trade in stock options.

Various Types of Options Chains

There are several different options chain formats available. These represent different options information. It is essential to learn a little more about the different formats in common use. This way, you will be conversant with them and be able to use any whenever encountered.

1. The Basic Call and Put Options Chain

Of all the chains available, the basic call and put options chain is the most basic. It is also the most widely used by investors and traders. This chain has a format that presents both put and call options with different strike prices on a screen. On the screen, you will observe information like the bid price, last price, ask price, open interest, volume, and open interest.

2. The Options Strategies Chain

This is yet another chain commonly used to present data on available options. This particular chain presents details of options within specific strategies. For instance, you will find a chain that presents the net debit of covered call options at various strike prices complete with relevant information such as assigned and static returns.

3. Call and Put Options Pricer

This particular options chain is more detailed compared to others. All the essential information is presented just like with other chains but also includes details such as the symbols. However, it showcases only call options or put options but never both. This makes it easier for a serious investor or trader to consult and get accurate information.

4. Call and Put Option Matrix

Finally, we take a look at the put options or call options matrix. This matrix endeavors to present numerous expiration months and strike prices on one page. The aim is often to present as many as is practically possible. Such a chain aims to provide users with as much useful data or information about call and put options as possible.

The Basic Call and Put Options Chain

This specific chain is generally the most popular options chain that is used by investors and traders, especially beginners. It is an excellent choice for those seeking to learn more about options.

This chain actually presents a split table with put options to the right and call options to the left. The different strike prices relevant to the options run fight down the center of the table. This way, investors and traders can easily track put and call options of various strike prices. This is demonstrated via the image presented below.

			Calls						Puts				
Symbol	Last	Chg	Bid	Ask	Vol	OpInt	Action	Strike	Symbol	Last	Chg	Bid	Ask	Vol	OpInt	Action
	Jan 10 Calls			(290 days to expiration)				BAC @ 7.8						Jan 10 Puts	
XOZAQ	0.21	-0.06	0.22	0.30	150	8,537	Trade	2.50	XOZMQ	1.41	0	1.28	1.39	00	22,515	Trade
WBAAZ	5.50	+1.25	5.60	5.80	401	4,817	Trade	2.50	WBAMZ	0.56	-0.14	0.53	0.57	1,322	40,939	Trade
XOZAA	0.05	0	0.03	0.05	263	15,588	Trade	5.00	XOZMA	3.60	-0.10	3.55	3.65	75	7,411	Trade
WBAAP	4.20	+1.20	4.15	4.30	1,616	26,895	Trade	5.00	WBAMP	1.64	-0.31	1.57	1.63	1,598	31,061	Trade
XOZAR	0.02	-0.01	0.01	0.02	41	38,850	Trade	7.50	XOZMR	6.26	0	6.00	6.20	00	2,991	Trade
WBAAQ	3.04	+0.94	3.05	3.15	2,149	75,590	Trade	7.50	WBAMQ	3.05	-0.40	2.92	3.00	531	19,620	Trade
XOZAB	0.01	-0.01	0	0.01	06	20,665	Trade	10.00	XOZMB	8.00	0	8.20	9.85	00	2,369	Trade
WBAAB	2.22	-0.72	2.21	2.25	2,179	57,337	Trade	10.00	WBAMB	4.60	-0.84	4.50	4.65	340	25,187	Trade
XPVAV	0.97	0	0.96	1.03	00	1,387	Trade	12.50	XPVMV	7.35	0	6.75	7.15	47	1,430	Trade
WBAAR	1.53	+0.50	1.54	1.60	849	47,231	Trade	12.50	WBAMR	6.75	-0.65	6.35	6.50	118	11,884	Trade
XOZAC	0.02	0	0	0.02	06	8,312	Trade	15.00	XOZMC	14.25	0	12.85	14.80	00	174	Trade
WBAAC	1.12	-0.41	1.10	1.12	1,037	36,741	Trade	15.00	WBAMC	8.65	-1.04	8.35	8.50	89	26,520	Trade
XPVAY	0.43	-0.09	0.42	0.48	37	1,305	Trade	17.50	XPVMY	11.90	0	11.15	11.65	00	3,374	Trade
WBAAS	0.74	-0.01	0.74	0.80	984	19,089	Trade	17.50	WBAMS	10.70	-1.20	10.50	10.70	312	13,426	Trade

Looking at the chain, we can observe that the strike prices run through the middle from top to bottom. We also note that the put options are located on the right side while the call options are on the left-hand side.

Other parameters such as bid price, last price, ask price, volumes, price change from the previous trading day and open interests are displayed for both put and call options. When it comes to trading or investing, this chain is actually the most widely used. It is popular with traders basically because it presents a lot of the information they consider crucial.

Important information necessary to execute trades is presented in a simple manner that is easy to read and understand. Using this chain, a trader can easily trace and identify available call and put options as well as other parameters affiliated to each option. However, this chain is most suitable for traders interested in simple options trading strategies. There are other chains suitable for more complex strategies.

The Call and Put Options Pricer

The put and call pricer is a chain that presents the necessary data relating to the basic call and put options. It also projects each option with five option Greeks. This way, an investor or trader who needs to use delta neutral options trading strategies and arbitrage strategies. The trader will be able to effectively make exact calculations regarding size and position to take.

Looking at a relevant chain, you will easily note that all the five Greek symbols that include Vega, Rho, Theta, Gamma, and Delta are used. They are visible in the call and put options pricer. However, due to challenges in full-screen presentations, options pricers usually present as either put options or call options only.

Options Strategies Chains

Specific options strategies chains are ideal for options traders or investors who prefer standardized options strategies like the covered call or the long straddle. The reason is because these chains drastically reduce the amount of work necessary to work out and calculate the options outlay as well as other specifics that relate to the specific strategy.

Options chains like this one generally present only the essential aspects of a particular options trading strategy across the various expiration dates and strike prices. This way, it is able to easily calculate and work out the net effect of a particular position and plenty of other useful detail. A trader is able to make quick decisions on the spread to choose fast without spending time doing calculations and working out arithmetic.

Call and Put Options Matrix

This particular chain is the least used by investors and traders, especially beginners and retail options traders. The aim of this chain is to present information on a large number of options including their bid and ask prices over numerous expiration dates all in one page.

This options matrix generally presents only the ask and bid prices for all options listed on the chain but without additional information. This makes it a less useful table especially for beginners, amateurs, and retail traders who basically need a lot more information. However, it is considered by many traders to be the least useful chain out there.

Learn About Options Pricing

Another useful aspect of options trading that you need to be familiar with is the aspect of pricing options. Option price is also known as the option premium and consists of two distinct components. These are the intrinsic value and the extrinsic value. Both are governed by the put-call parity principle.

What Are Extrinsic and Intrinsic Values?

We can define as the intrinsic value of an option as the value the option already possesses. This value is already present and contained in the option by the time you purchase it. Intrinsic value largely applies to call options

For instance, let us assume stock ABC is trading at a price of $50. If a call option is built into it and has a strike price of $40, then we can say that this option has an intrinsic value of $10 already built into it. This means that you will gain the right to purchase a stock worth $50 per share at $40 per share.

Extrinsic value is similar to intrinsic value but applies to put options rather than call options. Let us get back to our company ABC whose stock is still trading at $50. Now suppose that a put option is created on this stock but at a strike price of $60. This means that the option has an extrinsic value of $10 already built into it. In reality, you could immediately sell the stock at a price of $60 right after buying. An option that has intrinsic value is said to be in the money.

Calculating Intrinsic Value

To obtain the intrinsic value of a call option, you will simply deduct the call option's strike price from the stock's actual price or its prevailing market price.

Call Option Intrinsic Value = Stock (share) Price – Call Option Strike Price

An example:
Let us say that company ABC's stock is trading at $450, and its October $400 call option is asking for $50. The intrinsic value, in this case, is calculated by subtracting the call option strike price from the prevailing market price
$450 - $400 = $50.

In our case above, the intrinsic value of the call option is $50. Should this value be negative, it simply means that the call option has no intrinsic value and a put option has no extrinsic value.

Extrinsic Value

Extrinsic value can also be defined as the premium or time value of a put option. It is basically the part of the price that is determined by all other factors except for the value of the stock. The extrinsic value is actually the payment that you are making to the option seller to compensate for the risk that he or she takes for trading the options contract.

The money you are paying the trader or seller is referred to as risk money. The amount paid to the seller is considered justified and is essentially determined by a number of factors. These factors include dividends payable, volatility, interest rates, and expiration dates.

You will need a pricing model such as the Black-Scholes model if you wish to accurately determine the extrinsic value of any stock option, especially a put option. A stock's price is made up only of its extrinsic value in the event that there is basically no intrinsic value built into it.

Other Considerations of Stock Option Pricing

Sometimes, it can be tricky to price options when the prevailing market price of a stock and the option strike price are far apart. Such options generally have an extra layer or margin added to it partly due to unexpected large price movement and partly due to lower liquidity.

When pricing an option, there are a couple of other considerations that should be considered. For instance, if the underlying stock has a dividend payout and is payable prior to the expiration date. Another factor to consider is the prevailing interest rate. Should the general economic outlook call for interest rate adjustments, then this should be factored in when pricing options.

Strike Price
The strike price is a major component of any options contact. It also happens to be the sole static variable that affects an option's pricing. Each stock that can constitute an option has a different strike price and expiration date.

The strike price is typically determined using the stock's current market price. Take the example of a stock that is trading between $5 and $25. In this case, the strike price will vary with increments of about $2.50. The variations will be, for instance, $5, $10, $7.50 and so on. Let us assume that the stock price is trading between $25 and $200. In this instance, them the strike price will progress in increments of $25, $35, $40 or basically in increments of $5.

A strike price of any option is among the most basic determinants of the specific option that you will pick for trading purposes. For instance, if IBM stock is trading at $550 and has a good chance of rising beyond $570 in the coming months. In this instance, you may consider purchasing a $600 call option that has an expiration date of at least two or even more months.

Now when holding this option, you will have the right to purchase IBM shares at $600 even as other purchase at prevailing market rates. This is because the option contract that you hold has effectively secured you the right to purchase at the said price.

How to Price Options

Another factor that you need to be conversant with is how to price an option. It is important that you are able to price options correctly and accurately so that you do not incur unnecessary losses. The first step in pricing options is to understand all the elements that are involved.

Basically, the pricing process is a science and not an art. Once you master this science, you will be able to price options quite easily. Basically, options prices are determined by numerous external factors. However, 90% of the time, the price is influenced by volatility, stock price, and time till expiration.

Factors to Consider Include:

- Stock price
- Time
- Bid or ask price
- Volatility

1. Stock Price

When pricing options, the first place to begin is the market price of an underlying security. The security could be an index, a stock, or even ETF or electronically traded fund. This price is the predominant factor in determining the price of a stock.

Imagine Apple's stock trading at $500. The company then introduces a new gadget in the market. This new product is even greater than current gadgets like the iPhone. The shares then gain value and tend towards $550. In such an instance, a lot of shareholders will want to secure exclusive rights to buy the shares at $520. Basically, as the price of the shares goes up so do the call prices.

2. Time

Options are a factor of time. This means that they are wasting asset. In other words, their benefits are limited within a certain stipulated time period. This could be three months or six months. As an option approaches its expiration date, there is less time to benefit from it. As such, its value decreases proportionately. It is crucial that you always factor in time when pricing options.

3. Bid and Ask Price

Another crucial factor that plays an important part in option pricing is the bid or ask price. Basically, each option, regardless of whether it is a call or put, always has a bid and ask price.

Basically, when buying options, you will purchase at the asking price or very close to it and sell on the bid or very near to it. For instance, if you are looking at September 75 calls and notice prices like $9.60 x $9.90 then the asking price you'd be purchasing at is $9.90 while the selling price on this option has its lower margins at $9.60. The difference between these two prices that is the asking price and bid price is known as the spread. If the spread is very tight, then it means that the stock is very liquid.

4. Volatility

Yet another important factor that determines the price of an option is its volatility. In fact, volatility is the most crucial factor in the stock price. Basically, any options that are based on very long-term stable stocks will be predictably priced compared to options whose stocks have charts that are hugely volatile. Apart from past performance, implied volatility is also crucial so all these factors are considered when pricing a stock.

How to Read Options Quotes

One of the best sources for options quotes is the CBOE or the Chicago Board Options Exchange. If you visit the relevant website at cboe.com, you will come across the free twenty-minute delayed screen. However, for a small fee, you will receive real-time streaming quotes and general real-time quotes.

Option Volume and Open Interest

Two crucial pieces of options items that are related can be found marked on the quote. Volume refers to the total amount of trading activity recorded daily for a particular call or put option. Therefore, when a trader is buying or selling options, these will be recorded as part of the day's volumes. Volumes begin each day at zero and keep rising throughout the course of the trading day.

Open interest is basically a rolling tally of all the open and active options contracts at each strike. The number represents a total tally of all open and unexercised options. This figure does not necessarily change in the course of the day but adjusts itself overnight as soon as all exited positions are closed and the day's trades are tallied.

One challenge presented by the open interest is that it is very possible for it to remain unchanged or change just slightly. Some traders blame this on day traders who enter and exit positions. However, others think it's because options keep changing hands from one trader to another throughout the day. In any case, traders should always be on the lookout for the open interest and daily volume patterns.

Expiration Cycles

Any time that you are checking out securities with traded options, you are likely to note the different expiration dates as well as the changing patterns from one stock to another. As soon as a particular security begins to trade, it receives one of three random expiration cycles. This is simply due to the fact that there are numerous other securities trading at the markets that it would be a huge challenge to keep track of each call and put option at every strike price each and every month.

The three cycles commonly attached to options are:

- January, April, July, and October
- February, May, August, and November
- March, June, September, and December

Basically, the most crucial aspect to keep in mind is that there will always be options in the current month and options for the next month. An exception can only occur if a security is delisted from the exchange. Let us assume it is the month of May, and you wish to trade in company ABC's options. You will simply take a look at the May options and those available in June series.

You should also take a look at the options chain. This chain is available through your preferred broker. Remember that a chain lists options and the essential details of each option. You can also find the options chain on page one of Yahoo! and even Google. If you closely examine the top of such a chart, then you will note that there are options for May, June, July, and October.

Expiration Dates
You will also be expected to be on the lookout for options expiration dates. The benefit of trading options is that the aim is to trade and profit as fast as possible then exit a position. Profiting within a relatively short period of time and taking advantage of volatility is therefore quite common.

Ideally, options should expire each month on the third Saturday. However, since markets are not open on Saturdays, the expiry is moved to the third Friday of each month. Therefore, if you purchase an option in the month of July, then you can hold onto it until the third Friday of the month. Beyond this date, the option will not be profitable.

Within the relevant time period of your option, you are free to trade your option. You can, for instance, exercise your right to purchase the underlying stock or perform any other activity permissible with options.

Trading Options
Now that you are familiar about options terminology and characteristics, you can begin trading and making money. One of the easiest ways to do this is to simply buy call options.

How to Buy Call Options
When you buy a call option, you are also making a long call trade. This is a pretty simple and straightforward process. What you have to focus on is to take advantage of an upward trend in the market. Buying an option is considered the most basic and also the most popular way of investing in options. You will have a number of options once you purchase call options. These include:

- Selling the options,
- Purchasing the underlying stocks, and

- Allowing the option to expire.

Remember that when you invest in a call option, you receive the right to purchase the underlying stock. However, you are not obligated to do so. The reason why you invest in a call option is simply that you are of the opinion that the price of the underlying stock will rise. You will want to sell the option at a higher price than what you paid for in order to cash in and make a profit.

Buying Put Options

Apart from buying a call option, you can choose to buy a put option. This strategy allows investors and traders to earn profits on the downward trend. Put options generally provide opportunities to profit on the downside. Apart from profiting, buying put options allows you to hedge your stock if you expect them to lose value in the coming months.

When you invest your money in a put option, you earn the right to sell a stock at an indicated price. However, selling the stock is never an obligation on your part. Basically, if you are an investor, you would buy put options if you believe a stock is headed down in the coming days or weeks. In this instance, you will be exposed to a lower risk instead of shorting on the stock. This strategy can also offer you excellent liquidity as well as leverage.

Chapter 5: Risks That You Need to Avoid

Understanding Options Risks

Options trading process does carry some risks with it. Understanding these risks and taking mitigating steps will make you not just a better trader but a more profitable one as well. A lot of traders love options trading because of the immense leverage that this kind of trading affords them. Should an investment work out as desired, then the profits are often quite high. With stocks, you can expect returns of between 10%, 15%, or even 20%. However, when it comes to options, profit margins in excess of 1,000% are very possible.

Basically, these kinds of trades are very possible due to the nature and leverage offered by options. A savvy trader realizes that he or she is able to control an almost equivalent number of shares as a traditional stock investor but at a fraction of the cost. Therefore, when you invest in options, you can spend a tiny amount of money to control a large number of shares. This kind of leverage limits your risks and exposure compared to a stock investor.

As an investor or trader, you should never spend more than 3% to 5% of your funds in any single trade. For instance, if you have $10,000 to invest, you should not spend more than $300 to $500 on any one trade.

Also, as a trader, you are not just mitigating against potential risks but are also looking to take advantage of the leverage. This is also known as gaining a professional trader's edge. While it is crucial to reduce the risk through careful analysis and selection of trades, you should also aim to make huge profits and enjoy big returns on your trades. There will always be some losses, and as a trader, you should get to appreciate this. However, your major goal as a trader should be to ensure that your wins are much, much larger than any losses that you may suffer.

All types of investment opportunities carry a certain level of risk. However, options trading carry a much higher risk of loss. Therefore, ensure that you have a thorough understanding of the risks and always be on the lookout. Also, these kinds of trades are very possible due to the nature and leverage offered by options. A savvy trader realizes that he or she is able to control an almost equivalent number of shares as a traditional stock investor but at a fraction of the cost. Therefore, when you invest in options, you can spend a tiny amount of money to control a large number of shares. This kind of leverage limits your risks and exposure compared to a stock investor.

Time Is Not on Your Side

You need to keep in mind that all options have an expiration date and that they do expire in time. When you invest in stocks, time is on your side most of the time. However, things are different when it comes to options. Basically, the closer that an option gets to its expiration, the quicker it loses its value and earning potential.

Options deterioration is usually rather rapid, and it accelerates in the last days until expiration. Basically, as an investor, ensure that you only invest dollar amounts that you can afford to lose. The good news though is that there are a couple of actions that you can take in order to get things on your side.

- Trade mostly in options with expiration dates that are within the investment opportunity
- Buy options at or very near the money
- Sell options any time you think volatility is highly priced
- Buy options when you are of the opinion that volatility is underpriced

Prices Can Move Pretty Fast

Options are highly leveraged financial instruments. Because of this, prices tend to move pretty fast. Basically, options prices can move huge amounts within minutes and sometimes even seconds. This is unlike other stock market instruments like stocks that move in hours and days.

Small movements in the price of a stock can have huge implications on the value of the underlying stock. You need to be vigilant and monitor price movements often. However, you can generate profits without monitoring activity on the markets twenty-four hours a day.

As an investor or trader, you should seek out opportunities where chances of earning a significant profit are immense. The opportunity should be sufficiently robust so that pricing by seconds will be of little concern. In short, search for opportunities that will lead to large profits even when you are not accurate when selling.

When structuring your options, you should ensure that you use the correct strike prices as well as expiration months in order to cut out most of the risk. You should also consider closing out your trades well before expiration of options. This way, time value will not dramatically deteriorate.

Naked Short Positions Can Result in Substantial Losses

Anytime that your naked short option presents a high likelihood of substantial and sometimes even unlimited losses. Shorting put naked means selling stock options with no hedging of your position.

When selling a naked short, it simply implies that you are actually selling a call option or even a put option but without securing it using an option position, a stock or cash. It is advisable to sell a put or a call in combination with other options or with stocks. Remember that whenever you short sell a stock, you are in essence selling borrowed stock. Sooner or later, you will have to return the stock. Fortunately, with options, there is no borrowing of stock or any other security.

Chapter 6: Choosing a Broker

Mistakes that You Need to Avoid

As a trader, some of the mistakes that you will likely come across include overly aggressive positions, time decay, and unnecessary risks. However, there are other mistakes, and it is crucial that you avoid these as well. Many options traders, including seasoned ones, still make these.

Problems Pertaining to the Price Tag

There was advice once given to never buy something that you do not need simply because it is cheap. This advice is true for a lot of things including options positions. A lot of options traders, especially inexperienced or novice traders with little capital, are often attracted to the low prices pegged on deep, out of the money options. However, these often have a low chance of success. Avoid these kinds of mistakes. Basically, any option that is out of the money has a long way to go before it becomes profitable. It may run out of time, and you will probably lose money. Instead, think about costlier options that are in the money. You stand a much better chance at profitability with such options.

Manage Both Greed and Fear

As human beings, we are prone to emotions. These emotions are largely considered to be your worst enemy as a trader. You will notice that when a trade is having a good run, a lot of investors will be greedy and will not exit the trade according to a set plan. They will try and ride the upward momentum to milk it as much as possible.

Greed is also very visible when it comes to a downward trend. Ordinarily, traders should exit a trade when they start incurring losses.

There is no need to cling to a trade believing a turnaround is just a couple of minutes away. Some traders tend to overreact and bail out of trades the minute there is trouble. It is advisable to work out the ideal entry and exit points then use these to take profits or count losses then exit the trade. There is always tomorrow.

Having a plan is a basic requirement for all traders, whether amateur or experienced. Make use of the charts, examine your risk tolerance and also consider your goals as an investor. Once you have a plan, stick to it as much as is practically possible.

Properly Allocate Funds to Trades

You should allocate funds correctly to your trades. You do not want to allocate any amount above 5% of your investments to a single trade. Choose a number of trades and allocate each trade an amount between 3% and 5%. This way, you will stand to win a lot more than lose. You will also spread your risk and avoid losing all your money.

Let us assume that, as a trader, you have about $10,000 to invest in IBM shares. Now, assume that each IBM share costs $50. Therefore, instead of buying 200 shares, you should instead invest in options that ensure that you control 200 shares. This way, you will spend a lot less and stand to make just as much money. If 1 share has a premium of $2, then you will spend a total of $2 * 200 = $400 instead of $10,000. The remaining $9,600 can then be used to diversify your portfolio.

Identifying a Reliable Broker

There are plenty of brokerage firms available online. These brokerage firms provide traders like you with a platform to trade safely. These firms charge you a fee to access the platform and carry out your trades. They also provide you with tools that you need to trade successfully and customer service.

Generally, the lower the fees or commission charged, the less the customer service and assistance you can expect. On average, you should expect to pay between $2 and $5 per options contract that you invest in.

Sometimes you will be asked if you prefer a cash or margin account when opening an account with a broker. A cash account means you will trade using your own money. On the other hand, a margin account allows you access to credit facilities where you borrow money from the broker to invest in certain securities. Keep in mind that you are only able to borrow money from your broker against certain securities like bonds, stocks, and mutual funds.

You will not be able to borrow to invest in stock options because they are strictly cash-only trades. Options also settle trades the very same day or one business day. Therefore, you will require substantial cash amounts to enter trades. When you enter complex trades, you will also need to set some cash aside just in case you are obliged to buy shares at a certain price.

When opening an account, ensure that you choose a broker that rates you:

1. At this level, you are able to trade in options even as a beginner. Also, tick on the margin box rather than cash just so that you always have access to borrowing from the broker. There are generally four levels of traders. They range from level 0 to level 3.

At level 3, you are allowed to enter profitable but risky trades. For instance, you can participate in naked calls and naked puts. You can also participate in other more complex trades. However, risky trades will require much higher deposits so keep this in mind. All in all, brokers are all different. However, they will all need you to have access to cash and stocks in your account. This way, you will be able to fulfill your obligations and trade as often as you need to. Therefore, you will access options markets via your broker. Your broker will usually have access to the major platforms where options are traded such as the Chicago Board Options Exchange.

Conclusion

Thank you for making it through to the end of this book. Let's hope it was informative and able to provide you with all of the tools you need to achieve your goals whatever they may be.

The next step is to first try trading options on paper. This way, you will be able to visualize actual trades without losing any money. Try and build your confidence this way and then move to an online trade simulator. Here, you will trade just like you would on a broker's platform. However, you will use virtual money.

It is only after you are thoroughly versed with options trading, including common terminology, trading strategies, and so on that, you can now sign up with a broker and open a trading account. If you follow the instructions in this book, then you will begin making good profits in no time. Options are very lucrative and can make you wealthy if applied well.

Finally, if you found this book useful in any way, a review on Amazon is always appreciated!

www.ingramcontent.com/pod-product-compliance
Lightning Source LLC
Chambersburg PA
CBHW030513220526
45464CB00006B/2778